The Christmas Present

I Talk You Talk Press

Copyright © 2018 I Talk You Talk Press

ISBN: 978-4-909733-04-7

www.italkyoutalk.com

info@italkyoutalk.com

All rights reserved. No part of this publication may be resold, reproduced, stored in retrieval system, copied in any form or by any means, electronic, mechanical, photocopying, recording or otherwise transmitted without the prior written permission from the publisher. You must not circulate this publication in any format, online or otherwise.

This is a work of fiction. Names, characters, businesses, organizations, products, places, events and incidents are either the products of the author's imagination or are used in a fictitious manner. We have no affiliation with any existing companies mentioned in this story. Any resemblance to actual persons, living or dead, existing stories or actual events is purely coincidental.

Although the author and publisher have made every effort to ensure that the contents of this book were correct at press time, the author and publisher do not assume and hereby disclaim any liability to any party for any loss, damage, or disruption caused by errors or omissions, whether such errors or omissions result from negligence, accident, or any other cause.

Image copyright: © gtranquillity - Fotolia.com #58196761 Standard License

CONTENTS

Chapter One	1
Chapter Two	3
Chapter Three	4
Chapter Four	7
Chapter Five	9
Chapter Six	11
Chapter Seven	13
Chapter Eight	16
Chapter Nine	18
Thank You	20
About the Author	21

CHAPTER ONE

Kevin looks out of the window. Across the street, some people are putting Christmas lights up in their windows. Another family is putting a large Santa statue in their garden.

"Mum, can I put the Christmas tree up today?" asks Kevin.

"Yes, of course," says his mother.

"And can we put Christmas lights on the roof and on the windows?" asks Kevin.

"Yes, your father and I are going to do that now," says his mother.

Kevin's mother and father go into the garden and start putting up the Christmas lights. Kevin is excited. He loves Christmas. He puts some Christmas music on the CD player. He takes the Christmas tree out of the box. It is not a real tree. It is plastic and it is very big. He puts the Christmas tree next to the window.

If I put it next to the window, everyone outside can enjoy the tree too, he thinks.

He spends all afternoon putting decorations on the tree. Finally, he switches on the lights. The Christmas tree lights are red, yellow, blue and green.

This is wonderful! he thinks. *Now it feels like Christmas!*

He walks outside and stands in the front garden.

It looks good from the outside too, he thinks.

"Well done, Kevin," says his father. "That tree looks great!"

Kevin's father is in the garden. He is putting a large plastic snowman figure near the gate.

"I hope I can build a real snowman this year," says Kevin. "I hope we have lots of snow."

"I hope it doesn't snow today! I have to finish these lights!" says his mother.

Kevin looks up at the roof. His mother is on the roof. She is putting large Christmas lights up around the house.

Our house will look very bright, he thinks.

He looks around the street. Most of the other houses have Christmas trees and Christmas lights. There is only one house with no Christmas lights and no tree. Kevin looks at the house. It is very dark and there are no lights on.

"Dad, do you think Mr Evans will put his big Christmas tree up this year? Mr Evans' Christmas tree is always the best in the street."

His father stops working and looks across the road at Mr Evans' house.

"I don't know," he says quietly. "His mother went into hospital a few months ago. Maybe he is too busy."

"If I see him, I will ask him," says Kevin.

Kevin's mother comes down from the roof. "I've finished!" she says. "Let's switch the lights on!"

They switch the lights on. The garden and the house are very bright and colourful. "This looks great! This will be the best Christmas ever!" says Kevin.

"Come on, it's nearly time for dinner," says his mother. They all go into the house and close the door.

CHAPTER TWO

Across the road, Ben Evans is looking out of the window. He is looking at the other houses in the street.

It's Christmas time, he thinks. *My first Christmas alone.*

Ben Evans lived with his mother in the street for a long time. But a few months ago, she became sick and went into hospital. Ben went to visit her every evening after work. Ben has no brothers or sisters, so he had to look after her. She died a few weeks ago. Now he lives alone. His mother loved Christmas. She always put a very big tree up in the living room. The tree had many lights and was very bright. Everyone said, "This is the best Christmas tree in the street!" His mother was proud of the tree. Every Christmas Day, they had a big Christmas dinner, and ate Christmas pudding.

But not this year, thinks Ben, sadly. *For me, Christmas is cancelled.*

Outside it is getting dark. Ben can see Kevin and his family in their living room. They are eating dinner. They are laughing and smiling.

When I was a child, I loved Christmas, thinks Ben. *My mother and father didn't have much money, but they always made Christmas special. We always had a nice Christmas tree, and a big Christmas dinner. My mother loved Christmas too.*

Ben closes the curtains and switches on the light. Then he switches on the TV. Outside, all the houses are bright with Christmas lights. Ben's house is the darkest in the street.

CHAPTER THREE

It is Sunday.

Kevin goes outside into the front garden. He looks up at the sky.

"Why isn't it snowing? I want it to snow!" he says. "I want to make a snowman!"

He sees Mr Evans coming out of his house. He runs over to him.

"Good morning, Mr Evans!"

"Good morning, Kevin! How are you this morning?"

"I'm OK. But it isn't snowing!"

"No, maybe it won't snow this year."

"What do you think about my Christmas tree and lights?" asks Kevin.

"They look wonderful."

"Are you putting your Christmas tree up this year?" asks Kevin.

Mr Evans smiles sadly. He shakes his head.

"No, I don't think so."

"But your tree is great! It's the best tree in the street!" says Kevin.

"Maybe next year, Kevin," says Ben. "This year, for me, Christmas is cancelled."

"Cancelled? But you can't cancel Christmas, Mr Evans!"

Kevin cannot understand it.

"When you are older, you will understand," says Ben.

Kevin is not happy. "Adults always say that," he says.

Ben laughs. "Because it's true!" he says.

"Do adults always know more than children?" asks Kevin.

"Yes, we do," says Ben.

The Christmas Present

"But this time you don't," says Kevin.

"Why not?"

"Because you said 'Christmas is cancelled'. But you can't cancel Christmas, because Christmas is magic. You can't cancel magic. Do you believe in magic?"

"Well, I…"

"Kevin!"

Kevin turns around. His father is walking to them.

"Mr Evans is a busy man! Don't ask him so many questions!"

"Oh, it's OK, Mr Smith. It's always nice to talk to neighbours," says Ben.

Kevin runs into the house. He is not happy.

Kevin's father looks at Ben.

"How is your mother? I haven't seen her for a long time. Is she still in hospital?" he asks.

"Well, she died a few weeks ago."

"Oh, I'm so sorry. I didn't know," says Kevin's father.

"I didn't tell anyone," says Ben. "I was sad. I'm sorry I didn't tell you. I don't feel like celebrating Christmas this year. For me, Christmas is cancelled. I told Kevin, but he couldn't understand it."

"I'm sorry. I'll tell him about your mother. I hope he didn't upset you," says Kevin's father.

"No, no, he's just a young boy. He doesn't understand."

Ben says goodbye and gets into his car.

Kevin goes back into the garden and stands next to his father.

"What does he mean, I don't understand?" asks Kevin. "Adults always say that! But I am twelve. I understand a lot."

"Kevin, Mr Evans' mother died a few weeks ago."

"Died? But you said 'She went into hospital'," says Kevin.

"Yes, she did. Then she died. Mr Evans is very sad. Of course, he doesn't want to celebrate Christmas this year," says his father.

"Poor Mr Evans," says Kevin. "Does he have any other family?"

"I don't think so," says Kevin's father. "I don't think he has any brothers or sisters."

"What will he do on Christmas day?" asks Kevin.

"I don't know," says his father. "Maybe he will stay alone. Maybe he wants to be alone."

Kevin looks over at Mr Evans' house.

Christmas alone. That's really bad, he thinks.

Kevin's mother comes out of the house.

"Kevin! Do you want to come shopping with me? I'm going to buy a Christmas cake," says his mother.

"Yes! Let's go!" says Kevin. He gets in the car. He forgets about Mr Evans.

CHAPTER FOUR

On Monday morning, Kevin goes to school. It is the last day before the Christmas holiday.

He is sitting in class, talking to his friends. They are all excited about Christmas.

"What are you getting for Christmas?" he asks Dan.

"I'm getting an iPad," says Dan. "The newest iPad! What are you getting?"

"I want a new bike," says Kevin. "I want a mountain bike, so I can go to the countryside!"

"Good morning, children," says the teacher, Mrs Derby. "Today, we are going to talk about your Christmas homework. At Christmas, many people spend time with their family and have a good time. But some people don't enjoy Christmas."

"Don't enjoy Christmas? Why not?" asks Dan.

"Some people don't have any family. Some people feel sad and lonely at Christmas," says Mrs Derby.

Kevin thinks about Mr Evans. "The man across the road from me is like that. He said, 'Christmas is cancelled'. His mother died," says Kevin.

"That's right," says Mrs Derby. "People like that man. And there are many other people and many young children too. They are not excited by Christmas. They have a sad time."

The children were listening carefully.

"So, your homework is this. Do something nice for someone else. Find someone who is having trouble, and help them. Maybe you see an old person in town carrying heavy bags of shopping. Carry the bags for them. Maybe you see a homeless person in the town. Give them some food. Or, you can give a present to the local children's home, for children with no mother or father. Or bake cakes for a lonely neighbour. Do something nice for someone, and write a report about it. That is your homework."

Who can I help? thinks Kevin. *Mr Evans! Yes! He was sad. He cancelled Christmas. I can do something nice for him! But what can I do?*

CHAPTER FIVE

School finishes, and Kevin goes home. He puts the Christmas tree lights on and looks out of the window. He is getting very excited. He looks across at Mr Evans' house. His car is not outside the house.

He is still at work, he thinks. *What can I do for him?*

"Are you OK, Kevin? What are you thinking?" asks his mother.

"I'm thinking about my Christmas homework. Mrs Derby said, 'Some people don't have a nice time at Christmas.' We have to do something nice for someone, and write a report about it."

"That's a good idea. What are you going to do?" asks his mother.

"I'm thinking about doing something nice for Mr Evans. He will have a bad time this Christmas."

"That's nice, but I think you should leave Mr Evans alone. He is sad about his mother. He needs time. If he doesn't want to celebrate Christmas, that's OK. How about the old people's home? Many people in there are lonely. They have no family. You can bake some mince pies and take them. They will be very happy."

"That's boring. Everyone will do that," says Kevin. "I want to do something special."

"OK," says his mother. "You think about it. But you don't have much time left. It is Christmas Eve the day after tomorrow."

"I'll think about it," says Kevin. "Can I go carol singing with the other children tonight?"

"Of course you can," says his mother.

Kevin is happy. He likes carol singing. The children go to each house in the street and sing Christmas songs. The people in the houses enjoy listening to the children singing, and give the children mince pies, cakes, chocolate and hot drinks.

After dinner, Kevin and the other children go carol singing.

They knock on each door and sing Christmas songs. The people in the houses bring the children mince pies and hot cocoa. Some people give them money.

The children stop outside Mr Evans' house.

"He doesn't have a Christmas tree. And he doesn't have any Christmas lights up. Shall we skip here?" asks Brenda.

"Yes, let's skip here. Mr Evans has cancelled Christmas," says Kevin. "He doesn't want to celebrate Christmas this year."

"No, we can't skip here! The old lady in the house gives us nice chocolates every year. She gives us chocolates from Party Chocolate, that expensive shop in town. The chocolates are delicious!" says Paul.

"She's dead," says Kevin quietly. "So her son has cancelled Christmas."

Brenda and Paul are very surprised.

"That's too bad," says Brenda. "She was a nice old lady."

Mr Evans is sitting in his living room. He is looking through the curtains. He hears the carol singers.

My mother loved the children singing, he thinks. *She always bought chocolates for them.*

He watches the children go to each house. He listens to their voices and starts to feel sad. He looks around the room. He has a few Christmas cards from people at work, but the cards are still in the envelopes. He doesn't feel like opening them.

He puts the TV on, but all the programmes are about Christmas.

I'll go to bed, he thinks. *I can read in bed and forget about Christmas.*

CHAPTER SIX

The next day, Kevin wakes up early and gets ready. He is excited. He has an idea.

He has breakfast and puts on his coat and hat.

"Where are you going?" asks his mother.

"I'm going shopping," he says.

"Do you have any money?" asks his mother.

"Yes, I got some money last night when I went carol singing. Mr Rogers across the street gave us a lot of money!" says Kevin.

"Well, be careful. There will be many people out today. It's the last shopping day before Christmas."

"I'll be OK. I'll be back soon."

Kevin walks into the town centre. There are many people, and all the shops are playing Christmas music. He goes into Party Chocolate, and picks up a nice box of chocolates.

"Shall I wrap these for you?" asks the cashier.

"Yes, please," says Kevin.

"Who are they for?" asks the cashier. "Your mother?"

Kevin smiles. "They are for a friend," he says.

"That's nice."

Kevin buys the chocolates. Then, he stops to listen to a brass band in the centre of town. The brass band is playing Christmas music.

Cancel Christmas? I won't let Mr Evans cancel Christmas. I'll show him the magic of Christmas, he thinks. *Sometimes, children know more than adults!*

He goes to another shop and finds a very small Christmas tree. He buys the tree and some Christmas tree decorations.

He goes home. His mother and father are at work. He makes a cup of cocoa and looks out of the window at Mr Evans' house.

How can I get into his house? he thinks. *It's winter, so all the windows are closed.*

Then he remembers. Before the old lady went into hospital a nurse came to the house every day. The nurse used a key. The key was under the plant pot in the garden, next to the front door. *Is it still there? Mr Evans' car is not there. I think he is still at work. I can check now,* he thinks.

Kevin runs out of the house and across the street. He runs into Ben's garden and picks up the plant pot. There is a key under it.

Yes, the key is here! he thinks. He runs back to his house and closes the door.

CHAPTER SEVEN

It is Christmas Eve. Kevin is sitting in the living room with his mother and father. They are watching TV.

"Mum, Dad, can I hang my Christmas stocking up on the fireplace in the living room tonight?" asks Kevin.

His mother looks at him. "Why? You always put your stocking at the end of your bed. Santa comes into your room and puts your presents in the stocking."

"I know, but this time, I don't want Santa to come into my room," says Kevin.

"Why not?"

"Well, Santa has to carry my new bicycle. It will be very heavy. So he can put the bicycle and the other presents in the same place."

"That's fine," says his father. "We'll tell Santa not to go into your room."

Kevin looks at the clock. It is 9:00pm.

"I think I'll go to bed now. Christmas will come quicker if I go to bed," he says.

"OK, see you in the morning," says his mother.

"What time will you go to bed?" he asks.

"Probably around eleven," says his father. "After the film on TV has finished."

"What time will Santa come?" asks Kevin.

"After eleven," says his father.

"OK, goodnight," says Kevin. He goes up to his room and closes the door.

Kevin looks out of the window at Ben's house. The curtains are closed, but Kevin can see the light from the TV.

What time will he go to bed? he thinks. *I hope he goes to bed soon.*

Kevin starts to worry.

I hope my mother and father don't see me.

Kevin sits up in bed and tries to read a book. At last, he sees the lights in Ben's living room go out. Then, he sees Ben's bedroom light go on.

He's going to bed now, he thinks.

He waits a little longer. He hears his mother and father go into their bedroom. After a few minutes, the house is quiet. He looks out of the window. It is cold, but there is no snow yet.

The street is very quiet. After an hour, all the lights in the street go out. Everyone has gone to bed.

Now is the time! he thinks.

He picks up the small Christmas tree and chocolates. He opens his bedroom door slowly and quietly. He doesn't switch the light on. He has a torch. He walks very quietly down the stairs.

He stops at the bottom of the stairs and listens.

No, mum and dad didn't hear me, he thinks.

Then, he opens the front door very quietly, and walks out. Kevin is wearing his pyjamas, so he feels very cold. He runs across the road and into Ben's garden. He lifts the plant pot up and picks up the key. Quietly, he puts it in the lock. The lock turns with a click! Kevin doesn't move.

Did anyone hear that click? he thinks. *Everything is quiet. No, no one heard the click!* He opens the door very slowly and walks into Ben's house. He goes to the living room and puts the Christmas tree and present next to the window. Then, he walks out of the living room and out of the house. He closes the door very quietly, puts the key under the plant pot and runs back to his house.

Back in the house, it is very quiet.

He walks up the stairs in the dark. But then a light comes on!

"Kevin! What are you doing?" asks his mother.

Kevin puts the torch under his pyjamas.

"I needed to go to the toilet," says Kevin.

"You have to go back to bed quickly! Santa won't come if you are awake!" says his mother.

Then Kevin's father comes out of the bedroom. "Is everything

The Christmas Present

OK?"

"Yes, Kevin has just been to the bathroom," says his mother. "But he is going to bed now."

Kevin looks at them. "Why are you up?" he asks.

Kevin's mother and father look at each other. Then, his mother says, "I heard a noise. So I got up."

"Yeah, I heard your mother get up, so I got up too," says his father.

I was really quiet, thinks Kevin. *Did they really hear me?*

He goes into his bedroom, closes the door, gets into bed and falls asleep.

CHAPTER EIGHT

Ben Evans wakes up. He looks at the clock. 7:00am.

It's Christmas morning, he thinks. *I'll stay in bed for another hour. I don't have any reason to get up.*

He tries to go back to sleep, but he cannot. He looks out of the window. The Christmas lights on the other houses in the street are on already. Everyone in the street gets up early on Christmas morning. He can hear children laughing.

I'll get up and have breakfast, he thinks. *Then I'll watch a movie, or read a book.*

He gets up, gets dressed and goes down to the kitchen to make some coffee. He walks into the living room to open the curtains.

"What?" he says. He stops and looks at the Christmas tree and present. He stands looking at them for a long time. He cannot move. After a minute, he walks over to the present and picks it up. He looks around the room. Then, he runs to the front door and checks the lock. It's locked. He runs to the back door, and into every room in the house. He checks all the windows. They are all locked.

I don't understand it, he thinks. *Maybe I am dreaming.*

He goes back into the living room and opens the curtains. He picks up the present and opens it.

Chocolates from Party Chocolate! My mother loved these chocolates! She gave them to the children every year! But…who…why…

Ben looks around the room. He looks at a photograph of his mother. She is smiling in the photograph. Slowly, Ben starts to smile.

"Did you do this?" he asks the photograph.

Ben shakes his head. "I can't believe this," he says.

He picks up the small Christmas tree and puts it in front of the window. He looks at it for a few seconds.

No, he thinks. *I'll put it next to the window in the kitchen. It's too small for this window.*

Then he runs upstairs.

CHAPTER NINE

Across the road, Kevin is opening his presents in the living room. He has lots of presents. He has a new bike, some video games, books, and clothes. His mother and father are taking photographs of him opening his presents.

"Can I try my new bike?" he asks.

"OK, but put your coat on. It's cold outside," says his mother.

"And don't go too far. I'm making breakfast. It will be ready in about fifteen minutes," says his father.

Kevin puts his coat on and takes his bike outside. He looks across at Ben's house. There is a large Christmas tree in the window. Ben is putting lights on the tree. He sees Kevin and opens the window.

"Merry Christmas, Kevin!" he shouts.

"Merry Christmas, Mr Evans!" shouts Kevin.

Kevin goes across the road and stops outside Ben's house.

"I decided to put the Christmas tree up," says Ben.

"Why?" asks Kevin.

"Well, do you remember, you told me Christmas is magic?"

"Yes?"

"Well, I think you are right. It is magic!" says Ben.

Kevin smiles and cycles down the street. *I'll write my report about this tomorrow,* he thinks.

Kevin rides to the park. There are some other children riding bicycles, and some people are walking their dogs. Everyone says "Merry Christmas!" to each other.

Kevin looks at the sky. It is starting to snow.

The Christmas Present

Snow! Yes! he thinks. *Snow on Christmas Day! This is perfect!*

He goes back to his street and looks over at Ben's house. The lights on Ben's Christmas tree are shining brightly.

Kevin goes into his house. His father is looking out of the window.

"Look at that, Kevin. Mr Evans put his Christmas tree up. He decided to celebrate Christmas. But he is alone. I'm sure he will be sad today," says his father.

"Let's invite him to our house for Christmas dinner," says Kevin.

"That's a nice idea Kevin," says his mother. "Go and ask him."

A few hours later, Kevin, his mother and father and Ben are sitting around a table eating Christmas dinner. They talk about many things - work, living in the street, and Kevin's school.

"Did you do your homework, Kevin?" asks his mother.

"What homework do you have?" asks Ben.

"Kevin has to do something nice for someone," says his mother.

"Oh yes. I did," says Kevin.

"What did you do?" asks his mother.

"Er, well, I…"

"It's Christmas Day! Kevin doesn't want to talk about homework!" says his father.

"That's right. I don't want to think about school!" says Kevin.

Everyone laughs.

After dinner, Ben takes a box of chocolates out of his bag.

"Oh, chocolates from Party Chocolate," says Kevin's mother. "I love these chocolates!"

"Yes, these are very special chocolates," says Mr Evans. "They are a present from my mother!"

Kevin's mother and father look at each other, but they don't say anything. Kevin smiles. Everyone enjoys the chocolates.

Kevin looks around the table. *This is the best Christmas ever,* he thinks.

THANK YOU

Thank you for reading The Christmas Present! We hope you enjoyed the story. (Word count: 4,080)

There is a quiz about this book on our free study site I Talk You Talk Press EXTRA. http://italk-youtalk.com

If you would like to read more graded readers, please visit our website
http://www.italkyoutalk.com

Other Level 1 graded readers include
A Business Trip to New York
A Homestay in Auckland
A Trip to London
Dear Ellen
Haruna's Story Part 1
Haruna's Story Part 2
Haruna's Story Part 3
Ken's Story Part 1
Ken's Story Part 2
Life is Surprising!
Strange Stories
The Old Hospital
We Met Online

ABOUT THE AUTHOR

I Talk You Talk Press is a Japan-based publisher of language textbooks, graded readers and language learning/teaching resources.

Our team is made up of highly experienced language teachers and translators, who have all studied at least one additional language to an advanced level.

This experience enables us to design our materials from the perspective of both the teacher and the learner. We consult with both teachers and language learners when designing our textbooks and graded readers, and test our materials extensively in the classroom before publication.

We are a fast-growing press, and currently publish graded readers for learners of English. We publish new graded readers monthly.

www.ingramcontent.com/pod-product-compliance
Lightning Source LLC
Chambersburg PA
CBHW032006060426
42449CB00031B/853